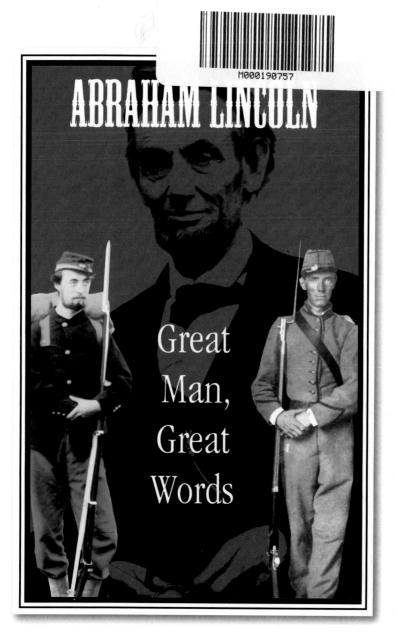

ABRAHAM LINCOLN

Great
Man,
Great
Words

Editorial Offices: Glenview, Illinois • Parsippany, New Jersey • New York, New York

Sales Offices: Parsippany, New Jersey • Duluth, Georgia • Glenview, Illinois
Coppell, Texas • Ontario, California • Mesa, Arizona

ISBN: 0-328-14390-1

Lincoln once worked as a "rail splitter." He split logs for building fences and cabins.

1. Lincoln Teaches Himself

President Abraham Lincoln is remembered for many things. One thing we remember is his wonderful way with words. When Lincoln talked, people stopped and listened. People stood in bad weather for hours to hear him speak!

How did Abraham Lincoln learn to read and write so well? Lincoln spent less than a year in school. He never went to college at all. But he was a great reader from the time he was very young.

Abraham Lincoln lived in this log cabin when he was young.

Lincoln was born in 1809. He and his family were **pioneers** who lived on farms in Kentucky, Indiana, and Illinois. Their **shelter** was a simple log cabin. Lincoln was too busy helping on the farm to go to school all the time. But he wanted to learn.

So what did he do? He borrowed books. He taught himself to read and write. He studied what he read. He taught himself math. When Abraham Lincoln decided to become a lawyer, he could not go to law school. So he taught himself law!

2. Lincoln Debates with Douglas

Lincoln worked as a lawyer for many years. He also worked as a Congressman, which means he spoke for the people of Illinois in government. When Abraham Lincoln gave speeches, many people came to listen.

In 1858 Lincoln ran for the United States Senate. He ran against Stephen A. Douglas. Lincoln asked Douglas to debate with him. A debate is a discussion about different opinions. Lincoln and Douglas debated seven times. Many people came to hear them speak. They talked mostly about slavery.

Lincoln was part of a group called the Republicans. Most Republicans thought that it was wrong for people to be **enslaved.** They hoped that someday it would end.

Big crowds came to hear Lincoln and Douglas debate.

Douglas was part of a group called the Democrats. In 1858 many of the Democrats did not agree with the Republicans about slavery. They thought that slavery should be allowed. They did not believe that slaves should have rights.

In the end Lincoln lost this election to Douglas. But the debates made him a famous man. Because he was such a great speaker, people wanted to hear what he had to say. When it was time to choose a man to run for President, the Republicans chose Abraham Lincoln.

These people escaped slavery and came to the North. Their stories encouraged people like Lincoln to work to end slavery.

3. Lincoln Talks About Slavery

The biggest topic in the Presidential election of 1860 was slavery. In the North, slavery was not legal. In the South, slavery was legal. Most people in the South were afraid that if Lincoln became President, he would try to take away their slaves.

Lincoln made many speeches about slavery. He tried to calm the fears of the people of the South. But he also made it clear that he thought slavery was wrong.

Lincoln was officially sworn in as President on March 4, 1861.

In his speeches, Lincoln said that slavery went against America's **tradition** of freedom. He knew that the Revolutionary War was fought so that the colonies could gain their **independence,** or freedom from English rulers. Lincoln was against slavery because he believed in freedom for all people.

The election was close. Many people were afraid of what Lincoln might do, especially in the South. But Lincoln won the election. He became President of the United States.

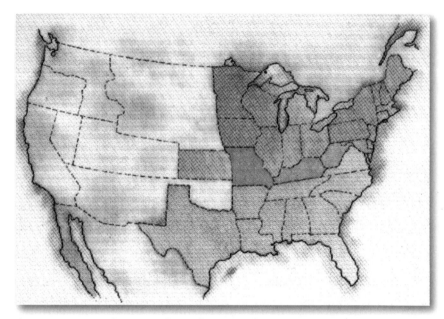

The green states on the map make up the Union. The purple states are the Confederacy. The four orange states stayed part of the United States, even though they allowed slavery.

4. Lincoln Talks to Southerners

Most of the people in the Southern states did not want Lincoln to be President. Some of them decided that they did not want to be a part of the United States anymore. They decided to start their own country. After the election, seven southern states seceded, meaning they broke away from the rest of the states.

Lincoln was very upset. He thought that it was not legal for a state to secede. Always a speaker, he tried to use words to convince the people of the South to change their minds.

Union soldiers wore blue uniforms. Confederate, or Southern, soldiers wore gray uniforms.

Lincoln tried to tell the South that the President was not allowed to take away their slaves, even if he wanted to. He said that in America it was tradition for people to work together even when they did not agree. He told them that he did not want to go to war. He said that the American people could find a peaceful way to end this disagreement.

Lincoln's speeches did not change things. In April of 1861 the North and South went to war. More southern states seceded. The North, called the Union, and the South, called the Confederacy, fought against each other. The Civil War had begun.

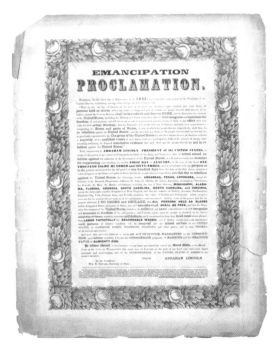

Lincoln's Emancipation Proclamation announced freedom for enslaved people.

5. Lincoln's Words During the War

The Civil War lasted from 1861 to 1865. Some of the most important things ever written by a President were written by Abraham Lincoln during the Civil War.

On January 1, 1863, Lincoln wrote and read the Emancipation Proclamation. Emancipation means "freedom," and a proclamation is a big announcement. With the Emancipation Proclamation, Lincoln said that all enslaved people in the Confederacy were now free.

Lincoln's most famous speech is the one he gave at the Gettysburg battleground.

On November 19, 1863, Lincoln went to Gettysburg, Pennsylvania, where a terrible battle had taken place. He gave a speech called the Gettysburg Address. In the speech he honored the people who had died in battle. Today this speech is thought to be one of the finest ever written by a President.

On December 8, 1863, Lincoln gave a speech about how the South should be treated after the war. In this speech he said that people of the South would not be punished, as long as they agreed to follow the law. He talked about his plan for bringing the Southern states back into the Union.

Lincoln spoke to his troops during the war. He thanked them for their help.

Lincoln also wrote many letters during the war. He wrote letters to the men in charge of the Union army. He wrote to family's of soldiers. Lincoln's letters showed that he was a wise, patient, and fair man.

In April 1865, the Civil war ended. The Union had won the war. Lincoln began to think about the big job of uniting the country again.

John Wilkes Booth shot Lincoln while Lincoln was watching a play.

Many people were still angry about the war and the end of slavery. On April 14, an actor named John Wilkes Booth shot Lincoln while the President and his wife were at a play. Booth thought he was helping the South. He just made it harder for the country to heal. President Lincoln died the next day.

The man who had spoken such beautiful words was now silent.

Thousands of people came to see Lincoln's funeral in Washington, D.C.

6. We Remember Lincoln

On December 6, 1865, the Thirteenth Amendment became a law in the United States. This law put an end to slavery in the United States. But even though the slaves were free, they were often treated poorly. Many people in the South stayed angry with the North. Some Northerners treated the South badly. The war was over, but the country was not peaceful.

But Abraham Lincoln had faith in the American people. He believed that in the end, they would do the right thing. He died knowing that our nation would live on, through good and bad times.

We remember Lincoln as the man who kept our country from splitting in two. We remember his thoughts and his ideas, and we remember his words. Maybe, like Lincoln, we can find ways to write and say things that make a difference in the world.

Glossary

enslaved: made to live as slaves, or people owned as property

independence: to be free from other people or places

pioneer: a person who goes first and prepares the way for others

shelter: a place where people live

tradition: something that is done a certain way for many years

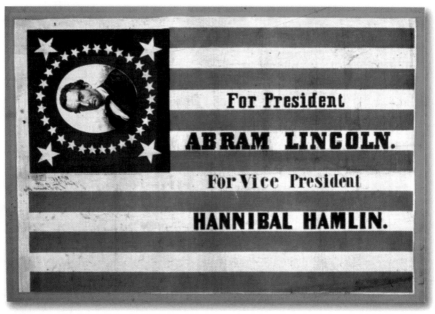

Political poster from the 1860 election